VANGUARD SERIES

EDITOR: MARTIN WINDROW

MODERN SOVIET COMBAT TANKS

Text and colour plates by

STEVEN J. ZALOGA

OSPREY PUBLISHING LONDON

Published in 1984 by
Osprey Publishing Ltd
59 Grosvenor Street, London W1X 9DA
© Copyright 1984 Osprey Publishing Ltd
Reprinted 1985, 1986 (twice), 1987, 1988, 1989

British Library Cataloguing in Publication Data

Zaloga, Steven J.
  Modern Soviet combat tanks.—(Vanguard series;
  37)
  1. Union of Soviet Socialist Republics. *Armiia*
  2. Tanks (Military science)—Soviet Union
  I. Title   II. Series
  623.74'752'0947   UG446.5

ISBN 0 85045 525 1

Filmset in Great Britain
Printed in Hong Kong through Bookbuilders Ltd

Author's Note:
The theme of this book is Soviet main battle tanks. Due
to the vast subject matter that this title encompasses, the
author has intentionally refrained from covering the
wide range of armoured support vehicles derived from
these types such as bridgelayers, armoured recovery
vehicles and engineer vehicles, in favour of covering the
extensive use these tanks have had in the many countries
which have purchased them. The author would like to
acknowledge the extensive support he has received on
this project, though many contributors must remain
nameless. He would especially like to thank Just Probst,
Pierre Touzin, George Balin, Simon Dunstan, Ron
Foulks, and Jim Loop for help in obtaining photos. He
would also like to thank Joseph Bermudez for help in
researching the Syrian markings shown in the illus-
trations; and Vika Edwards of the Sovfoto/Eastfoto
bureau for her patience while the author rummaged
through the photo files trying to locate various obscure
photos of Soviet and East European tanks.

Modern Soviet Combat Tanks

The T-44 first entered service in 1945 and was produced until 1947. This photo shows the improved T-44M in service in April 1977 on night manoeuvres. (Sovfoto)

The primary weapon of the Soviet Army and its Warsaw Pact allies is the tank. Since the end of the Second World War the Soviet Union has produced more tanks than the rest of the world combined, and has fielded an armed force which enjoys numerical superiority in tanks three- or four-fold over its potential opponents. This book is devoted to the main battle tanks developed by the Soviet Army since 1945, which in essence is the T-54/T-62 family and the succeeding T-64/T-72 family.

The T-44 Medium Tank

Plans were under way to develop a successor to the T-34 tank as early as 1941, under the designation T-34M. These efforts slipped into limbo when the Second World War broke out, due to the recognition by the NKTP (People's Commissariat for Tank Construction) that the only way that Soviet tank production could keep pace with the

staggering rate of battlefield losses was by concentration on the production of existing designs like the KV and T-34, to the exclusion of qualitative improvements. Resumption of work on a T-34 successor was not revived until 1944, by which time the war was going clearly in the Soviets' favour. The new tank was designed by the famous Morozov design bureau at Zavod Nr.183 in Nizhni-Tagil, and was designated the T-44.

The T-44 used nearly the same track, road wheels, engine and turret as the T-34/85. The main change was the hull configuration. The T-44 dispensed with the archaic concentric-spring Christie suspension of the T-34, in favour of a conventional torsion bar system which saved considerable internal space. The hull was considerably simpler in shape than the T-34, which simplified manufacture and reduced weight. In fact, the new hull was so much smaller than the T-

3

The first version of the T-54 to be produced in any quantity is shown here. It had a new turret design with a smaller pig-snout mantlet, but was distinguishable from the later, and standard, production model by the rear turret overhang. This particular early series T-54 is seen being transported over a river on a pair of tracked GSP amphibious ferries.

34 that the engine and its new transmission had to be mounted transversely. The turret was nearly identical to that used on the T-34/85 tank, but was thicker (up to 120mm of armour), and did not have the goose-neck turret ring. A prototype was completed in August 1944 and, after trials, the NKTP authorised limited production to commence at the re-opened Zavod Nr.75 in Kharkov. Design efforts were transferred to a team headed by N. Barykov, and some alterations were made in the design before quantity production finally started later in the year. About 150 or 200 T-44s were manufactured before the end of the war, and they saw limited combat in the final months of the fighting. The T-44 was one of the most advanced medium tanks to emerge from the Second World War. It combined extremely thick armour for its modest 32-ton weight, had excellent ballistic protection and good mobility. The usual Achilles

heel of Soviet tank designs, the transmission, proved troublesome in the initial production batches. An improved version, the T-44M was introduced on the assembly lines after the war, which corrected these defects and introduced other improvements such as a new, wider track which offered better flotation in soft soil and snow.

The T-54 Medium Tank

The main drawback of the T-44 was its retention of the same main armament as the T-34/85, the ZIS S-53 85mm tank gun. This weapon was not entirely adequate against German medium tanks like the Panther, and it was evident that the US and Britain were moving towards heavier armour on their new medium tanks such as the M26 Pershing and the Centurion. The frontal armour of these tanks was too thick to be penetrated easily by the 85mm gun at longer combat ranges. As a result, in 1945 a D 10-T gun was mounted in a modified T-44, known as the T-44/100. This vehicle proved successful in trials, but in the meantime it was decided to develop a new turret with a wider turret ring which could better absorb the recoil forces of the larger gun. This resulted in a prototype of the T-54 in 1946, and

production commenced in 1947.

The original version of the T-54 was short-lived and probably only a few hundred were ever built. The turret design of the initial T-54 series compared very unfavourably with other contemporary designs, notably the IS-3 heavy tank. As a result, a new turret was designed which eliminated the prominent shot-traps at the turret front, and substituted a small pig-snout mantlet for the wider mantlet of the initial series. This version of the tank, also called T-54, became the first variant of the T-54 series produced in any substantial quantity. This version was soon phased out in favour of an essentially similar version which had a slightly modified turret without rear turret overhang. This turret configuration was to become standard on all subsequent models of the T-54 and T-55 family. None of these types received any particular designation to distinguish them from one another—although here, the final type is referred to as the series production version. Due to the lack of common Soviet designations for the sub-types of the T-54 and T-55 family, US Army or NATO designations have been used here when appropriate.

This Finnish T-54 shows the main characteristics of the standard production model, notably the turret without rear overhang. This particular vehicle is armed with the earlier D-10T gun without the barrel fume extractor. The attachment points on the hull front are for the PT-55 mineroller kit.

The T-54 went through a number of product improvements during the early 1950s. A new version of the main gun, the D10-TG, introduced one-axis stabilisation. This was externally distinguishable by the use of a small muzzle counterbalance at the end of the gun tube. In 1955–56 a further improved type, known by the Soviets as the T-54A, was introduced. This used the same D-10TG gun as the final production run of the T-54, but had a fume extractor added to the gun tube to clear out turret fumes, which had proved excessive in the T-54. It also introduced a variety of other less noticeable features such as new road wheels, improved oil filters, a bilge pump, a fire extinguishing system, and power elevation for the main gun. A bilge pump had been added due to the development of a tank snorkelling system to allow tanks to ford rivers. Two years later the D-10TG gave way to the D-10T2S, which had two-axis stabilisation. At the same time, the new tanks

5

With the introduction of the D-10TG a counter-balance was added to the end of the barrel. Shortly afterwards a fume extractor was introduced which obviated the need for this counter-weight. This particular tank is a rebuilt T-55(M) on spring manoeuvres in the Leningrad Military District in April 1976. (Sovfoto)

were fitted for the first time with night-fighting equipment consisting of an L-2 infra-red searchlight for the main gun, a smaller OU-3GK searchlight for the commander, and suitable metascope sights. This version was called the T-54A(M) in Eastern Europe, though it is usually called the T-54B by NATO. After the adoption of infra-red night fighting equipment on the T-54B, many earlier models were retrofitted during their periodic overhauls. It should be kept in mind that Soviet tanks are generally rebuilt after about 7000km. At this stage, it is common for later features to be added to older model types. This results in initial series T-54s with later production wheels and infra-red gear, and makes it virtually impossible to distinguish the various production models of the later T-54s. These rebuilt vehicles with infra-red gear are sometimes distinguished T-54(M), T-54A(M), etc. by NATO, though it should be remembered that these are not their Warsaw Pact designations. The final production model of the T-54 series was the T-54C (also called T-54X). This was the first version to dispense with the DShK 12.7mm A/A machine gun mounted above the loader's hatch. On this version, a flush hatch was fitted over the driver's position.

The T-55 Medium Tank
In the late 1950s Morozov's design team began work on a re-engineered version of the T-54. Although the new version was nearly identical in

appearance to the T-54, a number of new internal features were added. Designated the T-55, it entered production in about 1959. Externally, the T-55 can be most easily distinguished by the absence of the prominent circular roof vent above the loader's station. In its place there is a small ventilation hole at the lower edge of the turret ring near the right side of the gun mantlet. Other minor exterior features include the use of a straight weld line where the glacis plate meets the lower bow plate; and many small changes on the engine deck.

The primary changes were internal. The T-55 was the first Soviet main battle tank to be fitted with radiation protection. This consisted of an RBZ-1M gamma ray detector which triggered a PAZ air overpressure system when a contaminated zone was entered. The 0.0015 kp/cm(3) overpressure kept contaminated air out of the fighting compartment. This was the first step in the Soviet Army's transition to tactical nuclear warfare, brought about by policy revisions under Khruschev; later

This T-54 provides a good example of the extent of rebuilding of older T-54s. The spoked wheels clearly point to the early production of this vehicle, yet it is fitted with many later features such as the rear fuel drum racks, infra-red night fighting searchlights and D-10TG or D-10T2S gun with fume extractor. It is also fitted with attachment points for the PT-55 kit, and is seen here on a training exercise in the Transcarpathian Military District in September 1975. (Sovfoto)

The T-54 was first used operationally in the suppression of the Hungarian uprising in 1956. Here, a Soviet T-54 is seen patrolling the streets of Prague during the invasion of Czechoslovakia in 1968. This T-54A is fitted with BDSh-5 smoke dispenser cylinders on the vehicle rear.

efforts included more extensive mechanisation of the infantry, in vehicles like the BMP, capable of fighting in a contaminated environment. The PAZ system also offers a measure of protection against chemical agents, but the primary motivation for its development was the doctrinal change anticipating the possibility of tactical nuclear warfare. At the same time, the T-55 was designed to ease preparation of the tank for underwater snorkel travel. The engine deck was revised to fit rubber sealed covers. This and other sealing measures were, of course, also related to the PAZ protection system.

The T-55 was fitted with the improved V-55 engine, which offered a modest boost in horsepower over the earlier V-54. The engine starting system was also improved. On the T-54 the engine is usually started electrically, with a compressed air back-up for use in cold weather and other conditions. On the T-55, the primary starting system is compressed air with electrical back-up; this was made possible by adding an AK-150 compressor for the air bottles to keep them replenished. The fighting compartment of the T-55 was considerably modernised, with new optics and with a re-arranged fuel and ammunition layout. A new front ammunition rack holding 18 rounds replaced the earlier 20-round rack; however, the new rack was built into a fuel tank which allowed additional fuel to be stored. The modified fuel racks allowed internal fuel stowage to go from 532l on the T-54 to 680l on the T-55, and ammunition stowage

increased from 34 rounds to 40 (finally to 43 on later models). The T-55 also had provision for stowing two 200l fuel drums on the rear, a hydropneumatically-boosted clutch, and a revolving turret floor.

In 1963 the T-55A appeared; this had further anti-radiation improvements added. This version had a special lead/foam lining panel added inside the crew compartment, and new, thicker hatches with anti-radiation liners. The T-55A also dispensed with the hull-mounted SGMT machine gun. Although neither the T-55 nor T-55A were fitted with the DShK 12.7mm A/A machine gun, in the late 1960s many were retrofitted with these weapons due to the continued growth of NATO's tactical ground-attack aircraft assets, and the deployment of tank destroyer helicopters like the US AH-1 Cobra gunship.

The T-62 Tank

When the T-54 and T-55 had been designed, Soviet tank divisions were configured with three tank regiments and a single heavy tank/assault gun regiment. This configuration stemmed from Second World War experience, which presumed that the medium tanks could tackle most enemy tanks, while the heavy tanks and assault guns could serve in the 'overwatch' role and engage enemy heavy tanks when they were encountered. However, by the mid-1950s it became evident to the Soviet Army that NATO tank forces were being built around much heavier and better-armoured tanks than had normally been encountered in the Second World War, such as the M48 and later mark Centurions. Although there were suitable HEAT anti-tank rounds available for the D-10 gun which could defeat these tanks, it has been Soviet policy to rely instead on kinetic energy rounds rather than chemical energy HEAT rounds, due to the use of primitive stadiametric sights on Soviet tanks, and to the rather limited live firing training of Soviet tank crews. HEAT rounds have a slow ballistic arc on their way to the target, which requires precise range-determination and extensive live round practice. In contrast, kinetic energy rounds have a nearly flat ballistic trajectory which requires little precise adjustment, and training can be done with much less expensive sub-calibre devices. The M48 and Centurion tanks had effective frontal thicknesses of about 200mm of armour. In contrast, the standard Soviet 100mm kinetic penetrator, the BR-412D APC-T, was capable of penetrating only 175mm of armour at the usual engagement range of 1000m.

To solve the problem, Soviet tank gun designers began work on a new family of guns called the *Rapira* (Rapier), which were smooth-bored and used sub-calibre finned projectiles with discarding sabots. The *Rapira 2* (2A20) 115mm towed anti-tank gun entered production in 1955, and work began on a tank version of the gun, the U-5T. While this was mounted on a T-55, it was decided that it would be prudent to mount the gun on a longer chassis which could better absorb the heavier recoil forces, and at the same time permit the stowage of adequate quantities of the larger ammunition. This resulted in the T-62, which entered production around 1961 at about the same time as the T-55A. The T-62 was heavily based on the T-55, and in fact used a great many components in common, such as wheels, track, engine and transmission, and even small features like the hatches and other fittings.

Apart from the new turret and lengthened hull, the only real change was the adoption of the 115mm gun. The U-5T firing the BR-5 APFSDS steel penetrator could punch through about 300mm of vertical armour at 1000m, which was adequate to deal with any contemporary NATO tank.

The T-62 was not a successor to the T-55 as is widely believed, but rather was its long-range counterpart. The T-62 was initially issued to independent tank regiments, while the T-54 and T-55 remained the bulwark of the tank and motor rifle divisions. This deployment scheme is reminiscent of the wartime practices with medium and heavy tanks, though the T-62 could hardly be considered a heavy tank in the class of the T-10M, which was beginning to be withdrawn from front-line service at the time. The T-62 could be used in the 'overwatch' role to cover the T-55s against heavier

Several of the Warsaw Pact countries provided token forces during the 1968 Czechoslovak invasion, such as this Polish T-54A(M), which carries the distinctive white cross air identification bands used during this operation.

NATO tanks. In later years, as more T-62s became available, they were also deployed like the T-55 in the tank regiments of the tank and motor rifle divisions. It is curious, however, that the T-62 was never adopted in anything but token quantities by the other armies of the Warsaw Pact. The reasons seem to be two-fold.

On the one hand, T-55 production was well under way in Poland and Czechoslovakia as well as the USSR, and as a result unit costs were very low compared to the T-62. For example, in 1970 when the Egyptians purchased T-55s and T-62s, they were charged only about 25,000 Egyptian pounds for the T-55, as compared to 250,000 roubles for the T-62. At current exchange rates that compares to about $57,500 for the T-55 to $172,500 for the T-62, although favourable exchange rates may have lessened this discrepancy somewhat. In addition, in 1968 the Soviet and Warsaw Pact units began to receive the new 100mm BR-6 HVAPDS round for the T-54 and T-55. This tungsten carbide penetrator could punch through about 264mm of vertical steel armour at 1000m, which is not significantly inferior to the performance of the steel BR-5 projectile. The main advantage of the BR-5 was that it was milled from steel, which made it considerably less expensive than the tungsten carbide BR-6. Finally, a new main battle tank was

The Chinese produce a copy of the T-54A as the Type 59, seen here during manoeuvres. These have been widely exported to Asia and Africa, and are virtually indistinguishable externally from their Soviet counterpart. (Simon Dunstan)

in development at this time, so it seemed pointless to deploy the expensive T-62 to the financially strapped Warsaw Pact satellites when a much better tank was expected to be available shortly.

As a result, T-55 production continued alongside the T-62, and even when production of the T-62 at one of the USSRs three tank factories was halted in favour of the new T-64, production of the T-55 continued. In fact T-55 production continued even after all T-62 production had been halted, not ending at Zavod Nr.13 in Omsk until 1979, and still continuing in Czechoslovakia and Poland to satisfy export requirements.

There were a number of production modifications on the T-55 and T-62 in the early 1970s. Like the modified T-55s with *Dushkas*, the T-62A was fitted with a modified turret and ring mount for the 12.7mm DShK A/A machine gun. Also during this

To assist in river crossings, Soviet tanks can be sealed and fitted with snorkels. Driving across riverbeds underwater is a tricky operation, as the tank retains some buoyancy and is difficult to steer. This formation of Polish T-55s are fitted with the Polish version of the underwater combat snorkel. A wider practice snorkel is sometimes used in training, wide enough for the crew to escape from a stalled tank. Note also that Polish T-55s have additional stowage boxes fitted to the left turret side. (Sovfoto)

period, a new 'live' track was developed which extended useful track wear from about 1,000–1,500km to about 2,000–3,000km and which reduced fuel consumption. This track can be retrofitted to older series vehicles by changing the drive-sprocket teeth ring.

Inside Soviet Tanks

The internal configurations of the T-54, T-55 and T-62 are essentially similar, and so these notes on the general interior are similar for all three tanks. The first thing one notices when inside a Soviet tank is its small size. Soviet tanks are designed around a crew no more than 5ft 6in tall, and the vehicle is very cramped even for such small crewmen.

In the front left side is the driver's station. Soviet drivers are officially called 'driver-mechanics', but in fact the driver has little training for maintenance aside from adjustments to the driving controls. The controls in Soviet tanks consist of two independent braking laterals (as on a tractor or Second World War tank), a five-speed clutch, and brake, clutch and accelerator pedals. Compared to contemporary NATO tanks, the driving controls of Soviet tanks are primitive and far more demanding. For example, in cross-country travel the driver must frequently shift gears and activate the clutch, while at the same time steering with the laterals. The complexity of steering is further encumbered by the lack of hydraulic boosting of the T-54 controls and by the often rough condition of the clutch. The controls are sluggish and require considerable strength and exertion, and an occasional deft mallet blow. In contrast, NATO tanks are no more difficult to drive than a car with manual transmission. Although the Soviet driver receives nearly as much training as his Western counterpart, much of it is on simulators rather than tanks, and the greater complexity of driving Soviet tanks requires considerably more practice. The main

This Czechoslovak-manufactured T-55A shows the primary characteristic of this variant: the larger hatch covers with improved anti-radiation lining. This particular tank of the CSA was taking part in Warsaw Pact manoeuvres around Doupov in June 1968 prior to the Soviet intervention. (Eastfoto)

reasons for the primitiveness of Soviet steering equipment are the perennial Soviet problems of shortcomings in transmission design, indifferent manufacturing standards on the working parts, and a general tendency towards simplicity in tank design even when it adversely affects crew performance. The combat implications of these features are driver inattentiveness to functions other than steering (such as monitoring vehicle instruments), premature exhaustion in cross-country travel, and increased tank breakdowns due to clutch failures. The advantage of such a configuration is that the tank is relatively inexpensive compared to its NATO counterparts, unless the life-cycle costs of clutch and transmission repairs are factored in.

To the driver's right is fuel and ammunition stowage. This is a vulnerable location for ammunition stowage, but given the very cramped interior of Soviet tanks there was no alternative. Besides the internal fuel and oil stowage, there are three 95 litre stowage panniers for fuel on the right fender, and an

Some T-55s have been retrofitted with a laser rangefinder, mounted externally above the main gun like these T-55s in operation in August 1978 in the Ciscarpathian Military District. These vehicles are also fitted with the improved 'live' track. Note the use of a geometric divisional insignia behind the three-digit vehicle tactical number. (Sovfoto)

external oil tank in various locations depending on the version of the tank. Since Soviet tanks run on diesel fuel, the external stowage of fuel is not as great a fire hazard as it would seem, though it certainly makes Soviet tanks more vulnerable to small-calibre autocannon fire than NATO tanks, which stow their fuel internally. The driver can adjust his seat to allow him to ride with his head outside of the tank, and an all-weather cover is provided on later model tanks, with a windscreen and windshield wiper. However, because of the low position of the main gun, the turret cannot be traversed if the driver's hatch is open without decapitating the driver. Communication with the rest of the crew is through an intercom system. There are throat mikes in the neck strap of the padded tanker's helmet, and the earphones are connected to a cord

The KMT-5 consists of a PT-55 mine roller assembly and the KMT-4 mine rake assembly. When it is in use the T-55 has its turret traversed rearward to prevent barrel damage during mine explosions, as demonstrated by this Finnish mine-rolling tank. In Soviet tank regiments nine sets of these roller assemblies are standard equipment.

which is plugged into the intercom box.

While there is no separation between the driver and the rest of the crew, neither is there any convenient access into the turret area. The turret is bisected by the gun, with the gunner and tank commander in the left half and the loader in the right half. Soviet tanks lack full turret baskets, so the crew sit on seats suspended from the turret race. Turret traverse is electrical with a manual back-up, which makes them about 30 per cent slower than NATO tanks using hydraulic traverse. This can be critical in close combat, but is not very important in long-range engagements. Soviet tanks since the early T-54s have power elevation for the main gun, and since the T-54B have two-axis

stabilisation. Evaluations of the quality of the stabilisation are not available, but Soviet crewmen have complained that the stabilisation system can be dangerous for the loader, as it can unexpectedly heave the gun about while the loader is attempting to locate or chamber a round. This problem is avoided in NATO tanks, since the floor of the turret basket traverses with the gun when the stabiliser actuates it[1].

The gunner virtually sits in the commander's lap in Soviet tanks. The firing procedure is for the commander to acquire a target through his designator sight, traverse the turret into a rough aim on the target, and provide the gunner with a target range and the loader with an ammunition selection. Once the gun is aimed and the round loaded, the commander orders the gun fired and the procedure is repeated until the target is hit or another target selected. The rangefinding control on Soviet tanks is a simple stadia system which consists of small lines in the commander's sight, with which he must measure the target and approximate

[1]T-55 and T-62 have traversing centre floors, but the ammunition racks are stationary.

its range. The system requires extensive training in order to be even marginally accurate, and, as a result, Soviet tank philosophy relies on kinetic energy projectiles which require little ballistic correction at ranges under 1000m.

The insides of Soviet tanks are cluttered with ammunition stowage. Besides the main bin beside the driver, there is ammunition stowed on the hull sides, under the gun and floor and on the rear turret walls. The loader has the least enviable task of all, since he must manipulate a projectile seldom weighing less than 50lb. within a very cramped space, dodging the main gun if the target is being engaged and tracked, and then ram the round into the breech with his right arm in a very contorted motion. Some crews use their left arm as a result of the poor layout of the turret. The severe space problems in Soviet tanks are an outcome of design requirements stressing volumetric limitation to keep down vehicle weight to a limit manageable by relatively small engines and transmissions. Larger vehicles inevitably necessitate more armour, more weight and larger engines, which raise vehicle cost. Taking the 1970 Egyptian example, at the time the T-55 was being sold for $57,000 and the T-62 for $172,000, the American M60A1 cost about $200,000. Small size also has ballistic protection advantages since it offers a smaller target to an opposing tank or missile launcher.

However, there are serious debits to reduced crew compartment size. To begin with, it drastically reduces ammunition stowage. Soviet tanks stow at least 50 per cent less ammunition than comparable NATO tanks, ranging from 36 rounds on the T-54 to 43 rounds on later T-55s, as compared to 60 rounds or more on the M60 series. It should not be forgotten that in the Second World War, Allied tank crews often felt that stowage amounting to up to 100 rounds was barely adequate due to the rapid depletion of ammunition in combat. A secondary problem with volumetric limitation is that it tends to reduce rate of fire. NATO tactics stress getting off the first round and firing quickly to cause rapid attrition in an attacking tank formation. Ideally, a tank crew should be able to get off three to four rounds in 15 seconds. While this standard is often reached in NATO crews, in Warsaw Pact crews a rate of fire only half as fast is commonplace due to inherent limitations brought about by the design as

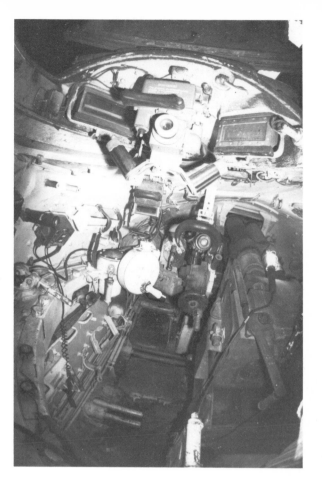

This interior view of the T-54 turret was taken from the commander's station. At the top of the photo is the commander's TPK-1 sight with vision blocks to either side. To the right is the breech of the D-10TG gun, while in the centre is the gunner's station with the gun and turret controls and the sight of the TShA-2-22 telescopic sight. The gunner's seat is not fitted in this view. This photo tends to exaggerate the amount of space in a T-54 as the tank is not fitted with ammunition stowage, which would fill part of the left side and cover the floor as well.

well as by lack of realistic training with live ammunition. The T-62 presents a special problem. The ammunition is so long and the turret so small that the gun must be raised to full elevation after firing to chamber the next round. This slows the reloading, and creates an ancillary problem. The system automatically ejects the spent casing out of the rear port, but in some cases the casing snags, misses the opening and bounces back into the cramped turret, seriously injuring the hapless crewmen. While the reduced height of Soviet tanks is a distinct advantage, it has forced the designers to place the centre of balance of the gun so low that Soviet tanks have very limited depression. This

This interior view looks forward into the driver's station on a T-54 tank, with the back of the driver's seat folded down. This view shows the basic steering laterals, clutch and control pedals as well as the various instruments and vision blocks.

severely limits the disposition of a tank in hull defilade as compared to NATO tanks.

In Soviet tanks the commander is in control of the radios. On the earlier tanks an R-113 radio was fitted, and in the newer vehicles, an R-123. These are clear voice FM radio transmitters, and are used solely for communicating or receiving communications from other tank or command vehicles in the unit. Soviet T-55K or T-62K command tanks have an additional R-112 radio which is used to communicate with neighbouring motor rifle units. These tanks have a special 10m antenna, and carry six rounds less of ammunition.

The final production runs of the T-55 were equipped with an externally mounted laser rangefinder above the gun, which offers increased accuracy at longer ranges. Some T-62s are being retrofitted with a similar system. The inherent

accuracy of the U-5T gun and fire controls were evaluated by the US Army using T-62s provided by Israel from war booty. The chart on p. 18 evaluates the probability of a T-62 hitting a tank-sized target at various ranges with the BR-5 kinetic energy steel penetrator round or with the BK-4M chemical energy HEAT round.

The basic gun tank version of the T-55 has been supplemented with a flamethrower version, the OT-55, seen here on manoeuvres in the Carpathian Military District in September 1982. This version has the usual PKT co-axial machine gun replaced by a flamethrower with external armoured mantlet, which can be seen to the left of the gun. The fuel is carried in place of the right hull ammunition stowage. (Sovfoto)

U-5T hit probability table

Ammunition	Rangefinder	Target	500m	1000m	1500m	2000m
BR-5	stadia	static	98%	79%	50%	27%
BR-5	laser	static	98%	86%	60%	43%
BR-5	stadia	moving	94%	75%	33%	19%
BK-4M	stadia	static	89%	69%	33%	11%
BK-4M	stadia	moving	75%	30%	5%	0%

As important as the inherent design of a vehicle is crew training. What figures like those in the chart

The Romanians have modernised their T-55s with a new suspension and possibly a new engine. This version, believed to be designated M-77, is seen on parade in Romania in August 1979. (Eastfoto)

fail to indicate is the quality of crew training and crew reaction in battle. Soviet training, like Soviet tanks, is very tight-fisted. Soviet crews get to engage in very little live ammunition firing during peacetime, in some units as low as three rounds per gunner per year, as compared to over 100 in many

NATO armies. Instead, 23mm sub-calibre devices are fitted in the barrel and used in the place of actual ammunition. While this is adequate for training the gunner, it does little to train for vital crew interaction in a combat situation.

Soviet tanks are designed and manufactured with clear limitations on durability. This is to some extent based on the very real appreciation of the short life expectancy of a tank in combat, and this design philosophy has been evident in Soviet tanks since the Second World War. It is also due to indifferent quality control. Soviet tanks generally require a major overhaul every 1,600km and a rebuilding at 7,000km. This reflects a much lower durability than NATO tanks. Soviet tanks like the T-62 are estimated to have a mean-time-between-failure rate of about 160–200km, compared to about 240–320km for the M60A1. The official life expectancy of a V-44 engine is 500 hours, but in some cases it has been as low as 100 hours due to poor workmanship. The limited durability of Soviet tanks inevitably puts severe constraints on peacetime exercises. In an average Soviet tank regiment only 12 of its tanks will be in use at any one time, while the remaining 88 are in storage. The training

Polish armoured engineer units use this local version of the UZR-3 mine clearing system in conjunction with the KMT-4 mine rake. The UZR-3 system consists of an unarmed 3M6 missile which is fired from a rear tub assembly, towing behind it a length of UZ-3 explosive hose. When the hose hits the ground it is detonated, clearing a narrow path about 500m long through a minefield by concussion. This particular version of the T-55 is known as the '*czolg rozgrodzeniowy T-55*'. In the Soviet Army this function is performed using a similar system mounted on a BTR-50PK or turretless SO-122 chassis.

tanks are periodically rotated, and every six months the stored tanks are taken out for a brief drive and servicing. While this technique limits undue wear on a unit's tanks, it also severely limits unit training above company size, and limits the time that crews actually train in a tank instead of on simulators. Carelessness over these durability limitations can have drastic effects in wartime. It is estimated that Egyptian T-54 units lost 80 per cent of their tanks due to mechanical breakdown in the 1967 war.

For all their faults, Soviet tanks are remarkably compact and effective weapons in the hands of a skilled crew. They are markedly less expensive than their NATO counterparts and this, as well as generous Soviet finance terms, have made them the most popular export tank since 1945, especially in

The IT-122 is an assault gun version of the T-55, mounting a 122mm D-74 gun. One battery of these guns is issued per motor rifle regiment, and they are used for direct, long-range fire support. An essentially similar vehicle, the IT-130, was also manufactured on the T-62 chassis, but mounting the 130mm M-76 gun.

the Third World, where tanks are more often used for parades or anti-coup forces than for combat.

The T-64 Tank

By the time the T-62 began to enter service in 1961, its new gun was already being challenged by the appearance of newer, more heavily armoured NATO tanks. The new M60A1 had frontal armour equivalents of about 250mm, which left the T-62 with a very uncomfortable armour penetration margin. The British Chieftain tank was even more heavily armoured. A second drawback in the T-62 tank was its relative lack of speed. Although the T-62 was comparable in mobility to the American M60, it was not fast enough to keep up with the new BMP infantry vehicle which was soon to enter service. Finally, the T-62, like all steel-armoured tanks, was vulnerable to a wide range of cheap anti-tank weapons like the US LAW rocket, the Carl Gustav, recoilless rifles, and a host of other weapons relying on shaped-charge, chemical energy war-heads. Furthermore, NATO, unlike the Warsaw Pact, tended to rely on shaped-charge HEAT rounds as their main anti-tank ammunition.

These three criteria—the need for increased tactical mobility, heavier firepower and better protection—led to the end of evolutionary development of the T-44/54/55/62 series in favour of a wholly new design: a heavier gun would require a larger and heavier chassis. These efforts culminated in 1967 with the introduction of the T-64 into service with the 41st Guards Tank Division at Kharkov. The T-64 incorporated an enlarged version of the U-5T gun, the 125mm *Rapira 3*. While this gun was no major departure from past Soviet tank design practices, almost everything else about the tank was. The suspension was a novel hydro-mechanical system which offered far better cross-country ride. The engine was of new design, apparently a five-cylinder opposed piston design generating about 800hp. Stadiametric rangefinding had given way to a coincidence rangefinder for better long-range accuracy. Most unusual of all, the crew had been reduced to three and an automatic loader introduced. There is also reason to believe that the T-64 incorporated an early form of laminate armour for added protection against HEAT rounds. The complexity of many of these features ran smack against previous Soviet design philosophy, which had stressed extreme austerity in the basic design. This philosophy was overridden by more pressing tactical requirements. The auto-loader, for example, was probably required in order to permit a minimal load of 40 rounds of ammunition to be carried. Given the usual Soviet requirements to keep size and weight low, had an autoloader not been used, ammunition stowage with a human loader would probably not have exceeded a derisory 25 rounds. Besides the *Rapira 3* gun, the Soviets also designed a gun/missile system somewhat akin to the US 'Shillelagh', which was called '*Kobra*'. It was mounted on a small number of T-64s, designated T-64B by the US Army.

For all its advanced features, the T-64 was apparently a real dog. In Soviet service it earned the nickname '*Stalovy grob*'—the Steel Grave. The initial dissatisfaction stemmed from problems with the autoloader. The turret space was so cramped that the autoloader would occasionally latch on to a crewman and hurl him into the breach, thereby generating sopranos for the Red Army choir. The suspension was excellent when functional, but was the subject of constant breakdowns, requiring the Zavod Nr.75 (Malyshev) at Kharkov to assign permanent engineering repair teams from the factory to the units which originally received the new tank. The gun's elaborate new fire control system did not prove to be adequate; and the engine, reputedly based on the troubled early Chieftain engine, was constantly breaking down.

The T-72 Tank

Like all weapons programmes, the T-64 had a momentum all its own, and thousands were produced while the designers promised to cure the bugs. Finally, in the late 1960s, it was decided to revert to the old ways and develop a more austere version of the T-64. The complicated suspension gave way to a conventional torsion bar suspension. The autoloader was retained but re-designed. The new engine was tossed out, and a turbo-charged version of the venerable V-2 diesel, used in Soviet tanks since 1938, was trotted out again. In 1971 the new tank, designated T-72, began replacing the T-64 on the assembly lines.

The first fuzzy photos of the T-64 turned up in 1974 in a film on Soviet winter manoeuvres. This was widely misinterpreted as an interim tank type, labelled the M-1970 or T-70[1] and supposedly consisting of a new hull with a T-62 turret. In 1977 the T-64 began turning up with the Group of Soviet Forces, Germany (GSFG), and as a result the US Army released the first clear photos of the T-64, though mislabelled 'T-72'. To further confuse matters, in October 1977 a visiting French military delegation was allowed to inspect a T-72 in the Moscow area, just before it was unveiled to the public in the November parade in Moscow celebrating the 50th anniversary of the Bolshevik Revolution. This morass of contradictory, inaccurate and confusing material led to a great deal of speculation regarding the evolutionary development of Soviet tanks, until more detailed material from defectors, intelligence sources, and the Soviets themselves began to clarify the matter.

Inside the T-72 Tank

There have been reports that British intelligence managed to obtain a T-72 manual in the mid-1970s, and there are even reports that several T-72s have managed to find their way into Western hands. Since the secrets of the T-72 appeared to have been compromised already, the Soviets have released more information on the T-72 than is usually the case. Nevertheless, unlike the other tanks described in this book, which the author has been able to inspect first hand, the following remarks are based on descriptive material from

[1] In fact the T-70 designation was apparently used by an aborted heavy tank project.

There are a wide variety of armoured recovery versions of the T-54 and T-55 tank, the earliest and most common being the BTS-2. This is basically a turretless T-54 with a box compartment in its place for equipment and winch stowage, and a large spade at the rear. In Polish service, as shown here, it is designated the WZT-1. It is being succeeded by a wide range of newer recovery vehicles with cranes and other features, such as the Czech MT-55, the Polish WZT-2 and others.

various sources, and there are likely to be gaps or erroneous information in the available sources.

The T-72 is a three-man tank weighing about 41 tons. Unlike the T-54 or T-62, the driver sits centrally in the hull, which eliminates the problem of having to lock the turret when the driver's hatch is open. The driver's controls are the same type of laterals used in the T-62, though there may be hydraulic boosting. To either side of the driver is fuel and ammunition stowage, but the glacis plate is so steeply angled that stowage in this area is far less vulnerable than in the T-62. The turret is bisected by the main gun, with the commander in the right half and the gunner in the left. Underneath them is a 'carousel' loader carrying 24 rounds of ammunition. The autoloader is apparently tabbed to permit the commander to select from three types of ammunition: high explosive, HEAT, or APFSDS kinetic energy penetrators. When cued by the commander, the carousel rotates until it first reaches the proper ammunition type. The tank stows about 40 rounds of ammunition, so when the carousel is depleted it must be reloaded from internal stores. The gunner's fire controls appear to consist of a coincidence rangefinder, which offers better long-range accuracy than the stadiametric system of the T-62. It is possible that the gunner is also afforded an image-intensification night sight on the later production batches of the T-72; but in any

A platoon of T-62 tanks take part in the October 1972 manoeuvres in the Siberian Military District. The lead tank is a T-62A with a mounting for the 12.7mm *Dushka* machine gun, while the other two vehicles are the earlier T-62 type without this anti-aircraft weapon. The tank at the top of the photo is using its TDA system to lay a smoke screen: this system works by feeding a small amount of diesel fuel onto the hot carburettor. (Sovfoto)

event, the tank uses a conventional infra-red night fighting array as well. The exact performance of the Rapier 3 gun is not certain, but US Army officers testifying before Congress have indicated that the APFSDS round is comparable in performance to the latest US 105mm M744 round, which means it is capable of frontally defeating any existing NATO tank, with the possible exceptions of the new generation of tanks with Chobham armour like the Challenger, M1 and Leopard 2. The turret has full gun stabilisation and hydraulic traverse. The new V-46 engine affords the vehicle superior mobility over the T-62, but probably not as great as originally reported.

The main enigma concerning the T-72 is the composition of its armour. Soviet sources claim that it is fitted with armour proof against anti-tank missiles, and a cross-sectional drawing appearing in

the Soviet military press shows a laminate armour in use. However, this laminate does not appear to be the same type as Chobham armour. The glacis armour on the T-72 appears to be about 200mm thick, while the improved Chobham armour on the M1 Abrams tank is apparently in excess of 500mm, though much of this is empty dispersion space. It would appear that the T-72 is armoured with an early version of laminate armour similar to that developed in the US in the 1950s for the T-95. It probably consists of a layer of conventional steel armour backed with a layer of ceramic to defeat the superheated gas tongue of a HEAT explosion.

Nevertheless, this armour is far from being invulnerable. In an interview in the IDF Journal, Maj.Gen.Moshe Bar Kochba, commander of the Israeli Armoured Corps, responded to a question about the Israeli experiences with the T-72 in the 1982 fighting in Lebanon:

Q: 'Though the present war proved that the T-72 is not invincible it seems that you have a great deal of respect for this tank (and perhaps even fear it).'

A: 'We don't relate to this tank in fear. We try to relate to it realistically. The T-72 is equipped with ultra-modern optical systems. Its strong firepower, penetrative, zeroing-in and destructive abilities are its most impressive features . . . As a result of our combat experience against it we have learned that the T-72 can be ignited and burns exactly like the T-62. It does not provide better armoured protection for its crew.'

In the 1970s development efforts continued on the T-72, resulting by the late 1970s in a new version probably designated T-74 (though called T-80 by the US Army). The main change introduced in this version appears to be in the turret fire controls, though other internal changes may have been incorporated. The T-74 lacks the right side optical port, presumably signalling the deletion of the optical coincidence rangefinder in favour of a laser rangefinder. This version also dispenses with the folding gill-armour skirts occasionally seen on the T-64 and T-72, in favour of a fabric armour skirt over the suspension and the sides of the external fuel cells. This added protection probably serves to protect the tank from side attack by current autocannons like the M242 25mm chain gun used on the US M2 Bradley Infantry Fighting Vehicle, which could probably penetrate the thin side armour otherwise. During training, the lower portion of these skirts is sometimes left off to give the crew better access to the suspension.

The first photos of the T-74 appeared in a Soviet military publication in September 1980, and an improved version of the tank with smoke mortars appeared in the November 1981 parade in Moscow. The T-74 became the centre of some minor controversy in the US in 1983 when a new edition of the Department of Defense publication *Soviet Military Power* was released with a photo of it from the November 1982 parade purporting to show the new 'T-80' tank. This conflicted with the 1981 edition of the same publication, which showed a 'T-80' with a boxy turret similar to that of Chobham-

A T-62A of a Soviet Guards tank regiment taking part in summer manoeuvres in the Western Ukraine in 1981. This tank is fitted with the KMT-4M or KMT-6 mine rake.

armoured tanks like the Challenger and M1. In contrast, the T-74 has the same cast turret as the T-72, though it may contain cavities with laminate armour.

The T-72 vs. NATO Tanks

In general terms, the T-72 is a generation behind the current crop of NATO tanks like the M1 Abrams, the Leopard 2 or the Challenger, having been developed nearly a decade before them. It is not as mobile as the M1 or Leopard; its armour is not as effective; and while its weapon is comparable in performance, its fire controls are more primitive, its rate of fire slower, and its night fighting ability more limited. For example, the T-72 is not fitted with a thermal night sight which would allow it to fight without any ambient moonlight on cloudy nights, or to fire its main gun accurately in the daytime through dust, haze or fog. This latter advantage of thermal sights should not be underestimated, as the considerable muzzle blast of modern tank guns tends to raise large clouds of dust when fired, obscuring the target to conventional optical sights.

Compared to older tanks like the American M60A3 or the German Leopard I, the match is somewhat better. The T-72 has comparable or superior mobility, better firepower and better armour. However, it has poorer fire controls, slower rate of fire, and the quality of its gun stabilisation system is undetermined. While the T-72 has very distinct tactical advantages over the earlier tanks, only combat can decide whether superior NATO tank crew training can counter-balance these advantages, in the way that Israeli crew advantages have often overcome the technical and numerical superiority of Syrian-manned Soviet battle tanks.

However, in spite of the current technical advantages enjoyed by newer NATO tanks over the T-72 or T-74, there is no reason for complacency. The Soviet Army enjoys a considerable numerical advantage in tanks over NATO, and it is unlikely that the T-74 is the last word in Soviet tank design. It should be kept in mind that the T-74 is nothing more than an improved version of the 17-year-old T-64, and it is entirely likely that an entirely new tank design is either in production or on the verge of production.

Soviet Tank Production and Export

The Soviet Union produces its tanks at three facilities, Zavod Nr.183 at Nizhni-Tagil, Zavod Nr.75 (Malyshev) at Kharkov and Zavod Nr. 13 at Omsk. In addition, Soviet tanks are produced in Poland and Czechoslovakia for Warsaw Pact requirements and for export. The USSR was still producing T-55s at Zavod Nr.13 as late as 1979, and derivatives of the T-55, such as armoured recovery vehicles, even later. The T-55 is still in production elsewhere in the Warsaw Pact at a rate of about 500 per year. The reason for the continued production of this nearly 40-year-old design is the considerable export market. In addition, it should be kept in mind that the Soviet Union, unlike most Western countries, tends to have both a high-cost and a low-cost tank in production at any given moment. In the mid-1960s the T-55 was the low end of the spectrum and could be used to bulk out the considerable Soviet Armoured Force, while the T-62 was also being produced to keep technically apace with NATO tanks. It would not be surprising to see the T-72 become the low end of the spectrum in this decade, with either a significantly improved version or a wholly new design making up the high end of the spectrum. The 'high-end' tanks tend to be issued first to independent tank regiments, and subsequently to the tank division's regiments and the motor rifle division's tank regiments.

Recent Soviet annual production of the T-72 and improved versions has averaged about 2,500 tanks per year. According to US Defense Intelligence Agency figures, 1970 was the peak production year with about 4,500 tanks being manufactured. In 1979 about 3,500 were manufactured. In contrast, the US is producing only about 800 tanks annually. The chart below, based on US DIA figures, provides a rough estimate of recent Soviet and Warsaw Pact tank production. ('C/P' indicates Czechoslovakia and Poland.)

Between 1973 and 1981, US sources estimate that the Soviet Union produced 23,000 tanks, of which some 13,000 were exported to the Third World. The primary clients have been the Arab states, which account for about 9,000 of these exported tanks. Further details of exports are as follows:

1: T-55, Czechoslovak Army; Vltava manoeuvres, 1978

2: T-55, Finnish 3./Tank Bn., 1981

A

37

1: T-55, B Sqn., Indian 9th Deccan Horse; Indo-Pakistan War, 1971

2: Type 59, A Sqn., Pakistani 11th Cavalry; Indo-Pakistan War 197

B

1: T-55 (M), Syrian 17th Mechanised Brigade; Kuneitra, 1967

2: Ti-67, Israeli Armoured Corps; Sinai front, 1973

C

1: Type 62, Chinese People's Army; Sino-Vietnam War, 1979

2: T-55 (M) of a Libyan tank battalion, 1981

D

1: T-54 (mod) of Maj. Saad Haddad's militia;
Sidon, Lebanon, 1982

2: T-55 (M) of an Iraqi tank regiment;
Basra, Gulf War, 1982

E

1: T-62A of an Afghan tank regiment, 1982

2: T-62, Soviet 11th Guards Tank Div.; GSFG, 1980

РЕВОЛЮЦИОНАЯ МОНГОЛИЯ

F

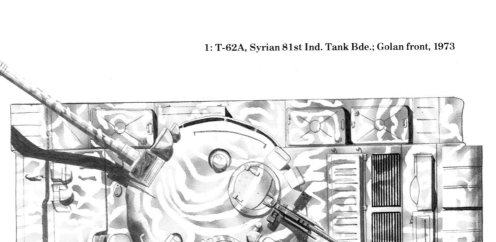

1: T-62A, Syrian 81st Ind. Tank Bde.; Golan front, 1973

2: T-62 of an Egyptian armoured brigade; Libyan border, 1979

G

1: T-72, Algerian Armoured Brigade, 1981

19790019

2: T-72 of a Czechoslovak tank regiment,
Druzhba manoeuvres, 1981

H

Soviet and Warsaw Pact tank production								
Type	Country	1976	1977	1978	1979	1980	1981	1982
T-55	USSR	500	500	500	500			
T-55	C/P	800	800	800	800	700	500	500
T-64/72/74	USSR	2000	2000	2500	3000	3100	2000	2500
T-72	C/P						20	100

Soviet Tanks in Service

Afghanistan: The Afghan Army began receiving 500 T-54 and T-55 tanks in 1962. This was followed in 1980 with initial shipments of about 100 T-62 tanks. The Afghan Army tanks have been extensively used, with little success, against the *mujhadeen* guerilla forces, who have disabled and destroyed many of them in spite of a lack of modern anti-tank weapons. Several T-55s have been captured by the guerillas, but due to lack of technical support they have quickly been abandoned.

Albania: Albania received about 15 T-54s from the USSR before breaking relations and siding with China. The Chinese connection brought in another 15 Type 59s, and reportedly some Type 62 light tanks as well, all of which seem to be attached to a single tank brigade.

Algeria: The Algerian Army received its first shipment of 50 T-54s in 1964, followed by additional shipments up to 1968, bringing the total to about 700 T-54s and T-55s. These were used to form an armoured brigade and three tank battalions. Shipments of T-62s, now numbering about 200, began in 1968, to permit the formation of a mechanised brigade along Soviet lines. An initial shipment of about 50 T-72s arrived in 1980, with more on order. Algeria's main defence concern is reportedly the situation in neighbouring Morocco; but the enormous tanks build-up by the neighbouring (and erratic) regime in Libya is probably also of concern.

Angola: Angola received about 150 T-54s and T-55s from the Soviet Union beginning in 1975, and later received 82 T-62 tanks. These arrived too late to take part in the fighting there, where tank support was provided mainly by Cuban-manned T-34/85s. There have been occasional encounters between Angolan armour and South African forces.

Bangladesh: Bangladesh had about 30 T-54s or T-55s donated by Egypt in 1974, but their operational status is dubious.

Bulgaria: The Bulgarian Army is organised on Soviet lines with eight motor rifle divisions and five tank brigades, equipped with 2,100 T-54/55s and about 100 T-62s. The Bulgarians were one of the few Warsaw Pact armies to receive any number of T-62s.

China: China received a small number of T-54s before the break with the Soviet Union, and apparently was given assistance in producing a copy of the T-54A, the Type 59. The Chinese have produced in excess of 10,000 Type 59 tanks, which form the mainstay of the nine to twelve armoured divisions and the tank battalions of the infantry divisions. They have been exported in sizeable numbers, and saw combat with Pakistani and Vietnamese forces. They have also been employed in the border wars with Vietnam. In 1969 the Chinese began manufacturing the improved Type 69, which is basically a Type 59 with a new gun derived from the Soviet U-5T 115mm gun captured during border fighting with the Soviets in the 1960s along the Ussuri River. Probably the most unusual variant of the T-54 to have emerged in China is the Type 62 light tank, a thinly-armoured, scaled-down version of the T-59 armed with an 85mm gun. China has exported its tanks extensively, and in the period from 1977 to 1981, 3,500 tanks were built and 810 of these were exported.

Congo: The Congolese Army fields one armoured battalion equipped with a platoon of 12 PT-76 scout tanks, a platoon of 15 Type 59 tanks, and a platoon of 14 Type 62 light tanks. The Congo also received 35 T-54s or T-55s from the Soviet Union.

Cuba: The Cuban Army has received about 400 T-54/55s from the Soviet Union beginning in 1963,

The T-64 first entered Soviet service in 1967, and here a unit is seen participating in the Zapad-81 manoeuvres in summer 1981. This is the later version on which the remote-control machine gun was removed from the commander's hatch. The T-64 can be distinguished from the later T-72 by its suspension and rear engine deck, but in a frontal view the location of the infra-red searchlight on the right turret side most clearly distinguishes it.

and these were followed by about 60 T-62s in 1975–76. Cuban tank troops have seen action in Angola, and have been used in a training role in other Third World countries.

Czechoslovakia: The Czechoslovak Army (CSA) received its first T-54 tanks in the early 1950s, and production of the T-54 began at Martin after 1956. For a time the T-62 was also produced, but this was mainly for export. T-72 production began in 1981. Czechoslovak tanks have been widely exported through the Soviet Union, especially in the Middle East. The CSA is organised along Soviet lines and fields the 1st, 4th, 9th, 13th and 14th Tank Divs. and the 2nd, 3rd, 15th, 19th Motor Rifle Divs.; its 3,600 T-54/55s are mostly locally produced, and it has about 100 T-72 and T-74 tanks. The CSA was ordered to refrain from fighting in the 1968 invasion, but Czech tankers insist that had fighting taken place, the CSA units would have 'walked all over' the Soviet tank units due to far better training. *Egypt:* Egypt received its first 120 T-54 tanks in 1956 to rebuild the 4th Armd. Div., which had been decimated in the 1956 war with Israel. Additional T-54/55s were received to fill out this unit and to equip the 1st Mech. Bde. Both units were committed to the Sinai front in the 1967 war, where they suffered from severe mechanical problems owing to the fact that they had been driven long distances before the fighting began without adequate repair time. Both units were gutted by the Israelis, and 291 T-54s and 82 T-55s were lost. Following the war, the Egyptian Army purchased 1,260 T-54s and T-55s and 400 new T-62s. Although the Egyptian forces fought far better in the 1973 war against Israel, they again suffered massive tank losses on the Suez Front.

A further 600 T-62s were purchased after the war, but under President Sadat Egypt broke relations with the USSR and sought reconciliation with Israel. As a result, Egypt is saddled with a large inventory of Soviet tanks, numbering about 850 T-54/55s and 750 T-62s, without a source of spares. Several Western firms have begun manufacturing spare parts and ammunition for the Egyptian tanks as well as modernisation kits. One of the more ambitious projects is the programme by the Royal Ordnance Factories in Britain to develop a 105mm gun mounting for the Egyptian T-55s. A prototype was completed and shipped to Egypt in 1982, and it is likely that modernisation efforts on Egyptian tanks will continue. Since 1973 Egyptian tanks have been engaged in periodic border clashes with Libyan tanks. (For further details of Egyptian use of Soviet tanks in the 1967 and 1973 wars, see Vanguard 19, *The Armour of the Middle East Wars.*) *Equatorial Guinea:* The forces of President-for-Life

26

Nguema were overthrown in 1978, and a handful of T-54/55s took part in the coup. The source of these is unknown.

Eritrean Liberation Front: The ELF has about 50 T-54/55s which were probably turned over to them by Arab governments sympathetic to their struggle with Ethiopia. These have been used in the war in small numbers.

Ethiopia: Ethiopia received about 500 T-54/55s from the Soviet Union and they have seen extensive use, both in the war against the ELF, and in the war against Somalia in the Ogaden Desert. The intervention of Somali-backed guerilla forces in the Ogaden fighting in 1977 led to increased Soviet support and major counter-offensives in 1978. In January and February the Ethiopian Army launched a number of attacks supported by about 120 T-55 and T-62 tanks. In February 1978 Somalia formally entered the war, but heavy Soviet backing plus the support of Cuban troops overwhelmed the Somali forces. In July the Ethiopians turned on the ELF, but were not as successful in routing out these guerilla groups, which are still engaged in the war to liberate Eritrea. Ethiopia reportedly received 40 new T-72 tanks in 1982.

Finland: The Finnish Army has a single armoured brigade equipped with over 100 T-54 and T-55 tanks. About a third are the older T-54s.

Germany (DDR): The East German Army (NVA) fields the 7th and 9th Panzer Divs. and the 1st, 4th, 8th and 11th Motor Rifle Divs., organised along Soviet lines. Its primary equipment is the T-54 and T-55, with about 2,500 having been obtained from the USSR, Poland and Czechoslovakia. It was the first Warsaw Pact country to receive the T-72 in any number, and was the first with the newer T-74. These currently number in excess of 100 tanks.

Guinea: Guinea has a single tank battalion with about 15 T-34/85 tanks and about 25 T-54/55 tanks.

Guinea-Bissau: Guinea-Bissau has a single tank battalion with about 15 T-34/85s and 30 T-54/55 tanks.

Hungary: The Honvedseg fields the 2nd and 5th Tank Divs. and the 35th and 102nd Motor Rifle Divs.; Hungary has about 1,490 T-54/55 tanks, and in 1979 began receiving an initial shipment of about 80 new T-72s. Hungarian units are organised on

Soviet lines, but usually receive new equipment after the German NVA, the Czechoslovak CSA or the Polish LWP.

India: Following the 1965 war with Pakistan, India turned increasingly to the Soviet Union for military equipment. In 1968 the Indian Army began receiving shipments from Czechoslovakia of 225 T-54 and 225 T-55 tanks. At the time of the outbreak of the 1971 war with Pakistan, India had one armoured division and five independent armoured brigades. The T-54 and T-55 were the principal equipment, numbering about 450 tanks, with a further 200 Centurions, 300 Vijayantas, 150 AMX-13s and various other older tank types. The Indian T-54/55s were used on both the front with Pakistan and in Bangladesh, though in the latter theatre the

The T-72 has been exported to most of the countries of the Warsaw Pact, including the German NVA, as seen here. (P. Touzin)

PT-76 proved handier owing to the large number of waterways.

Tank fighting during the 1971 war was complicated by the fact that the Pakistani Army was heavily equipped with the Type 59, so it was difficult to distinguish friend from foe. As a temporary solution most Indian T-54s and T-55s had a large tin can attached mid-way down the barrel to mimic the fume extractor on the L7 105mm gun used on the Vijayanta and Centurion. Many also had a 55gal. drum attached to the rear of the turret. Some vehicles also had a .30cal. Browning machine gun added on a pintle mount in front of the loader's hatch.

There were two major armoured engagements on the western front. In the Punjab, the Indian 2nd and 16th Armd. Bdes. tangled with the Pakistani 6th Armd. Div. and 8th Armd. Bde., equipped with M47 and M48 Pattons, and some old Sherman tanks. Early in the fighting T-55s fitted with mine trawls proved useful in clearing initial Pakistani

28

The latest version of the T-72, the T-74M, is also called the 'T-80' by US Army sources. It is basically the same as the T-74, but has a bank of smoke mortars added to either turret side. These vehicles are on parade in Moscow in November 1981. The T-74 is in use with the German NVA; the T-74M is in use with the Czechoslovak CSA and is presumably entering production there. (Sovfoto)

minefields, but the soft terrain soon put an end to their usefulness. In the fighting on 15–16 December the Indians claimed to have knocked out 45 Pakistani tanks, mainly Pattons, while admitting only 14 losses. There was another smaller armoured engagement in the Chaamb area, and this is covered below in the section on Pakistan. The only other major tank-vs.-tank combat came on the eastern Bangladesh front. The only substantial Pakistani armoured force in Bangladesh was the 29th Cavalry, equipped with 72 badly worn out M-24 Chaffee light tanks. These were broken up into small groups for infantry support, and were wiped out or captured by Indian anti-tank teams, PT-76s or T-55s. During the 1971 war the Indian Army admitted losing 69 tanks: 24 in Bangladesh, 38 in the western sector, and seven in the south during the Rann of Kutch fighting. The Indian Army continued to modernise after the 1971 war, with a current inventory of about 950 T-54/55s. The Indian Army is currently modernising some of

The T-72 was succeeded by the T-74, which uses an improved fire control system and incorporates other improvements. These T-74s on exercise in the Carpathian Military District in September 1982 show some of the differences encountered on vehicles which have been deployed with the troops for some time. The gun barrel has the thermal protective sleeve removed, and the tanks have the lower portion of the fabric armoured skirt removed, though the upper portion remains. (Sovfoto)

the T-55s by installing an L7 105mm gun. In 1978 India ordered its first 70 T-72 tanks, and more are likely to follow, with production in India possible.
Iran: In 1982 Iraq charged that the Soviet Union had secretly transferred 62 Soviet tanks to Iran to help in the Gulf war. It is unclear if this is true, or simply a case of Iran using some of the many Iraqi tanks previously lost during the fighting that broke out in 1980, or purchased from Israel.
Iraq: Iraq began purchasing T-54 tanks from the Soviet Union in 1959, acquiring about 80 that year, and subsequently acquiring about 1,000 T-54/55s, 1,500 T-62s and about 100 T-72s. During the 1973 war the Iraqi 3rd Armd. Div. was sent to help Syria, but was ambushed by Israeli tanks and lost about 80 of its 310 tanks in a brief but bloody firefight. At the outbreak of the 1980 war with Iran the Iraqi Army fielded four armoured and two mechanised divisions and one independent armoured brigade. These units have apparently suffered heavy losses, though details are lacking. The war strained relations with the Soviet Union and the Iraqis have

The T-54A first entered Afghan service in 1962, and many have been lost in the fighting with the *mujhadeen* guerilla fighters. (P. Touzin)

turned to other sources for tanks, including Poland and China. The Chinese reportedly sold Iraq 130 Type 69 tanks in 1982, with a further 130 to be delivered in 1983. Poland apparently supplied a modest number of T-55s.

Israel: Israel captured several hundred T-54/55s and T-62s during the course of the 1967 and 1973 wars. After the 1967 war the IDF rebuilt about 200 T-54/55s using the L7 105mm gun, and incorporated other small improvements such as American radio gear and machine guns. These were designated Ti-67, and were used in the 1973 war. Some of the unconverted T-54s and T-62s were sold to the US after 1973 for use by US OPFOR training units. During the fighting in Lebanon in 1982 a further 91 tanks and APCs belonging to the PLO or to Syrian forces were captured intact.

Kampuchea: Vietnam has given its allied Kampuchean forces a small number of Type 62 light tanks.

Laos: Laotian forces were given a small number of T-54 tanks, probably by Vietnam in the early 1970s.

Lebanon: The forces of Maj. Saad Haddad were reinforced with several dozen refurbished T-54/55s in 1982 by Israel. These vehicles had stowage bins added to the turret and other modifications, but were not re-armed with the 105mm L7 gun like the Israeli Ti-67s.

North Korea: The North Korean Army fields two armoured divisions, four to five armoured regiments and ten tank training battalions. The bulk of

this force is made up of Soviet T-54/55s and Chinese Type 59 and Type 62s. There are also about 200 T-62 tanks in use, and North Korea is beginning local production of this tank, presumably with some supply of parts from the Soviet Union.

Libya: Although the Libyan Army supposedly fields only 12 tank battalions, it has a massive inventory of some 2,000 T-54/55s, 750 T-62s and 150 T-72 tanks purchased from Soviet, Czech and Polish sources. Some of this inventory is used to supply Islamic allies. The Libyan tank force has been used during the border fighting with Egypt and during the invasion of Chad in 1980. In Chad the Libyans used about 70 tanks in half-a-dozen companies to support infantry attacks on N'Djamena. The number of Libyan tanks greatly exceeds the number of trained crews.

Mali: Mali has about 25 T-54/55s and six Chinese Type 62 light tanks, a large proportion of which are probably unserviceable.

Mongolia: The Mongolian Army is believed to field a single armoured brigade with about 100 T-54/55 tanks.

Morocco: The Royal Moroccan Army acquired 35 T-54/55s from the USSR in 1962 and a further 80 from Czechoslovakia in 1967–68. They have been employed in the war with the Polisario guerillas, and several have turned up in Polisario hands. They are being phased out in favour of modern Western equipment.

Mozambique: Due to continued outbreaks of fighting with South Africa, Mozambique expanded its tank force with the purchase of 100 T-54/55s in 1979 and another 50 in 1980, bringing the total to about 200 tanks. About 160 T-62s were reportedly ordered as well. There have been a number of clashes with South African forces, and the Mozambique forces have lost a number of tanks.

Nicaragua: Nicaragua reportedly received 25 T-54/55s from Cuban stores in 1982.

Nigeria: Nigeria has expanded its tank force to cope with border troubles with the Cameroon and Chad, including the purchase of 80 T-54/55 tanks in 1979. These apparently equip the 22nd Armd. Bde. of the 2nd Mech. Div., and have been retrofitted with British night sights and radios.

Pakistan: After the 1965 war Pakistan turned increasingly to China for its armoured vehicles. When the 1971 war broke out it had about 50 T-54s

and 225 Type 59s in addition to its American equipment. The only major fighting involving these tanks took place on the western and southern sectors of the front. One of the largest confrontations involving the Type 59 tank took place in the Chaamb sector, where the 11th Cavalry (with full regimental strength of 44 Type 59s) and the 28th Cavalry (which, being a recce regiment, had only 31 tanks), along with about 55 Shermans and M36s in other units, took part in fighting against the Indian 72nd Armd. Regt. and 9th Deccan Horse. The Indian regiments were both equipped with T-54/55s and, together with an independent AMX-13 squadron, totalled 104 tanks. These forces were heavily engaged in the fighting for the Mandiala Heights on 4 December, with a particularly sharp engagement between the 11th Cavalry and Deccan Horse. Chaamb was captured on 7 December, and the Pakistanis claimed the capture of 13 T-54/55s plus the destruction of 20 others, for a loss of 10 Type 59s, seven Shermans and two M36s. The Pakistanis felt that the Indians had a distinct technical advantage in the tank fighting, as the Indian T-54s and T-55s had infra-red nightfighting equipment that the Type 59 lacked, and had the improved BR-6 ammunition, while they had to rely

During the 1971 war with Pakistan Indian T-54s and T-55s had a metal cylinder added to the gun barrel to mimic the L7 105mm gun and distinguish themselves from the similar Pakistani Type 59 tanks. This T-54A was knocked out by Pakistani forces during the Chaamb fighting, and belonged either to the 9th Deccan Horse or 72nd Armoured Regiment. It shows the full set of insignia on the hull glacis plate consisting of the bridging circle ('37') in yellow, the serial ('UX934'), and the British-style regimental insignia ('371' on a red/yellow square). (Col. M. Durrani via G. Balin)

on the Chinese equivalent of the old BR-412D round. Pakistani units emerged less successfully from fighting around Longewala on 4/5 December, losing 37 Type 59s, mostly to air strikes. The Indians claimed the destruction of 276 Pakistani tanks in 1971, though the bulk of those lost were the M24s in Bangladesh, and American types lost around Shakargarh. Pakistan currently fields about 700 Type 59s which make up a part of the strength of two armoured divisions and four armoured brigades.

Peru: Peru's one armoured brigade and supporting armoured units are made up mostly of 250 T-55s purchased from the Soviet Union in 1973. About 150 more were ordered in 1982 to make up for the heavy mechanical breakdown rate of these tanks.

Poland: Poland fields the largest tank force in the Warsaw Pact, including the 5th, 10th, 11th, 15th,

An Iraqi armoured unit prepares for combat in the Dezful area west of Kharkeh on 30 March 1982. The bulk of the tanks are T-62As; to the left is an MT-55 armoured recovery vehicle, manufactured in Czechoslovakia on the T-55 hull.

16th and 20th Tank Divs. and the 1st, 2nd, 3rd, 4th, 8th, 9th, 12th and 15th Motor Rifle Divs. Polish units are organised along Soviet lines, and are equipped mainly with T-54 and T-55 tanks manufactured in Poland. Polish T-54s and T-55s, like the Czech versions, tend to be more durable than their Soviet counterparts due to better workmanship, and often incorporate improvements not carried on the Soviet tanks. The Polish Army (LWP) began to receive T-72s from the USSR in 1979, and will probably manufacture the T-72 in place of or in conjunction with the T-55.

Romania: The Romanian Army fields two tank and eight motor rifle divisions, equipped for the most part with some of its 1,670 T-54/55 tanks. In the late 1970s Romania began rebuilding these with new running gear, a new engine and other improve-ments. This version is believed to be called the M-77. In 1979 Romania bought 30 T-72s from the USSR.

Somalia: The Somalis bought 100 T-54/55s in the 1970s and 70 T-62s, equipping three armoured brigades. However, during its involvement in the Ogaden War with Ethiopia mentioned above, it lost at least 60 T-54/55s and probably about 40 T-62s. The remainder will probably fall into disrepair due to Somalia's break with the USSR.

South Africa: The South Africans have at least 12 T-55s confiscated from a Libyan shipment to one of their neighbours, and possibly additional vehicles acquired in border raids. Their employment is unknown.

Sudan: The Sudan was courted by the USSR in 1968–71 and was sold 70 T-54s and 60 T-55s. However, relations went sour after an attempted Communist coup in 1971, and subsequently 30 Type 62 light tanks were acquired from China in 1972 before the government reverted to its pro-Western stance.

Syria: Syria began to receive its first T-54s and T-55s after the 1964 'Water War' with Israel. During the 1967 war three T-54 and T-55 units were involved in the fighting: the 17th Mech. Bde. with a battalion of T-54/55s, and the 14th and 44th Armd. Bdes. each with three battalions of T-55s. The 17th Mech. Bde. saw the heaviest fighting, and lost several of its T-54/55 tanks to the Israelis. Generally Syrian tank losses in this war were modest, however, amounting to only 73 tanks of all types. By the time of the 1973 war the Syrian units had been entirely re-equipped with T-54/55s or newer T-62s. The Israeli defences on the Golan Heights were very nearly overrun by the Syrian armoured and mechanised units, but held by the slimmest thread. This story is told in more detail in Vanguards 19, *Armour of the Middle East Wars*, and 22, *The Centurion Tank in Battle*.

Syria fields about 1,500 T-54/55s, 900 T-62s and about 250 T-72s, with a sizeable fraction stationed in Lebanon. There have been discussions between Syria and a British consortium to rebuild the older T-54/55s with new fire controls, and possibly engines and armament. The Soviet T-72 saw its operational debut with the Syrian 3rd Armd. Div. in the Bekaa Valley fighting in 1982. The Syrians lost about eight T-72s to Merkavas of the Israeli 7th Armd. Bde., and possibly some more to airstrikes. The Syrians claim that an Israeli column of about 30 armoured vehicles was wiped out by a T-72 unit, but this has not been confirmed by any other source, and Israeli tank losses in Lebanon were very modest.

A Polisario guerilla stands beside a knocked-out Moroccan T-54A. The Polisario guerillas have captured a number of T-54s, and since other T-54s and T-55s have been obtained from Libya they can field up to 50 of these tanks.

Tanzania: Tanzania fields a single tank battalion with 22 Type 59s received in 1971 and 20 Type 62s received in 1967. Tanzania also has about 350 T-54s originally intended for ZAPU forces in Rhodesia before the civil war ended, but these apparently have not been absorbed by the army yet. The Chinese tanks were used by Tanzania during its intervention in Uganda in April 1979.

Uganda: Idi Amin purchased about 15 T-54/55s, but all of these were lost during the 1979 war with Tanzania.

USSR: The Soviet Army currently fields 52 tank divisions and 117 motor rifle divisions, and possesses the world's largest tank force. It consists of about 1,500 T-44s, 20,000 T-54/55s, 13,000 T-62s, 3,000 T-64s and 10,000 T-72/74s. A Soviet tank division under the new re-organised table contains three tank regiments and a motor rifle regiment, totalling 328 tanks at full strength. A motor rifle division under the new tables fields three motor rifle regiments and a tank regiment, and totals 220 tanks at full strength. These figures do not include the host of other armoured combat vehicles.

Vietnam: North Vietnam received both Soviet T-54 and Chinese Type 59 tanks during the course of the war. Neither type was known to have been encountered by US tanks, and the first South Vietnamese engagement with T-54s took place on 19 February 1971 in Laos around fire base LZ31. The NVA forces eventually took the position, but not until ARVN M41A3 tanks had destroyed many. ARVN forces continued to run into T-54s

A formation of Libyan T-55s on parade in Tripoli in 1981. The presence of a stowage bin on the left turret side indicates that these tanks are of Polish or Czechoslovak manufacture. The tank to the left has the name 'Saladin' on the turret.

throughout the remainder of the war, particularly after the March 1972 Easter offensive. During the attacks on An Loc alone the ARVN destroyed about 80 of 100 tanks engaged, consisting mostly of T-54s and Type 59s. The NVA learned from its mistakes, and in the 1975 offensive which overwhelmed South Vietnam T-54 and Type 59 tanks played a prominent role. (Further details of these battles can be found in *Vietnam Tracks* by Simon Dunstan, Osprey, 1982.) T-54, Type 59 and Type 62 tanks were also used by Vietnamese forces in the Cambodian invasion, and during the border war with China in 1979. Vietnam is believed to have about 500 to 800 T-54/55/59 tanks and reportedly received 200 T-62 tanks in 1972.

Yemen: North Yemen bought about 100 T-54/55s from Poland, and South Yemen (PDRY) acquired 100 T-54/55s in 1972.

Yugoslavia: Although not a part of the Warsaw Pact, 900 T-54/55s make up the bulk of the Yugoslav armoured force.

Zaire: Zaire's small tank force consists mainly of armoured cars and 38 Type 62 light tanks obtained from China.

Zimbabwe: Zimbabwe has a small number of T-55s captured by Rhodesian forces from Mozambique.

Soviet Tank Tactical Turret Numbering

The Soviet Army does not appear to have a standardised tactical numbering system in its tank regiments, though certain styles are common, and those shown below are typical. Number* indicates a battalion commander's tank; number† a company commander; and number‡ a platoon leader. As can be seen, under this system the first digit indicates the battalion, the second the company and the third the vehicle. In other units the first (1 to 3) indicates the regiment within the division, the second the company (from which the battalion can be deduced), and the third the vehicle. Each company consists of three platoons of three tanks, plus a company commander's tank. Within a tank division, the second and third regiments would use subsequent numbering (i.e. 400, etc., for the first battalion of the second regiment).

Regt. HQ	100
1st Bn. HQ	101*
1st Co.	110†, 111‡, 112, 113, 114‡, 115, 116, 117‡, 118, 119
2nd Co.	120†, 121‡, 122, 123, 124‡, 125, 126, 127‡, 128, 129
3rd Co.	130†, 131‡, 132, 133, 134‡, 135, 136, 137‡, 138, 139
2nd Bn. HQ	102*
4th Co.	240†, 241‡, 242, 243, 244‡, 245, 246, 247‡, 248, 249
5th Co.	250†, 251‡, 252, 253, 254‡, 255, 256, 257‡, 258, 259
6th Co.	260†, 261‡, 262, 263, 264‡, 265, 266, 267‡, 268, 269
3rd Bn. HQ	103*
7th Co.	370†, 371‡, 372, 373, 374‡, 375, 376, 377‡, 378, 379
8th Co.	380†, 381‡, 382, 383, 384‡, 385, 386, 387‡, 388, 389
9th Co.	390†, 391‡, 392, 393, 394‡, 395, 396, 397‡, 398, 399

The Plates

A1: T-55, Czechoslovak Army; Vltava manoeuvres, 1978
The Czechoslovak Army is the only Warsaw Pact army which regularly uses pattern-painted camouflage. There are several schemes available for different seasons, the one illustrated consisting of sand, rust brown and white added over the usual dark green. There does not seem to be any regular pattern to the colours, which are apparently applied at the discretion of the crew or unit. The inset drawings above show the Czechoslovak national insignia to the left and the Polish national insignia to the right.

A2: T-55, Finnish 3./Tank Battalion, 1981
Although Finnish tanks were painted, up to 1980, in overall dark green, there have been recent experiments with pattern-painted camouflage, in

A Pakistani Type 59 tank knocked out by airstrikes in the Longewala area on 4-5 December, 1971. A Pakistani regiment attacked the border post at Rajasthan with Type 59s, and lost 37 to air strikes and Indian tanks in the battle that ensued. (Chris Foss)

is case using black and a medium green (FS 34102) over the usual dark green (FS 34077). These colours are applied in a harsh, segmented pattern. The Tank Bn. pennant consists of three yellow arrows on a background of company colour: black, red or green. It derives from the Second World War sleeve and cap badge of the Finnish Armoured Division.

B1: T-55, B Squadron, Indian 9th Deccan Horse; Indo-Pakistan War, 1971

This view shows some of the distinctive features added to Indian T-55s to distinguish them from Pakistani Type 59s, notably the tin can on the barrel and the extra fuel drum on the turret rear. Although the Indian Army apparently has a system of pattern-painted camouflage, during the war the

Technical Data

	T-54A	*T-55A(M)*	*T-62A*	*T-72*
Weight (tonnes)	35.5	36	40	42
Crew	4	4	4	3
Length overall (mm)	9000	9000	9335	9240
Hull length (mm)	6040	6200	6630	6950
Width (mm)	3270	3270	3300	3490
Overall height (with mg)	2750	2700	2745	2770
Height w/o mg	2400	2350	2395	2370
Basic fuel stowage (litres)	817	965	960	1000
Added fuel stowage (litres)	0	400	400	400
Max. road range (km)	440	715	700	650
Max. terrain range (km)	290	500	450	450
Max. road speed (km/h)	50	50	50	60
Max. gradient (degrees)	30	30	30	30
Trench crossing (m)	2.7	2.7	2.8	2.8
Vertical obstacle (m)	0.8	0.8	0.8	0.8
Engine type	V-54	V-55	V-55	V-46
Horsepower	520	580	580	780
Power/weight ratio (hp/t)	14.4	16.1	14.5	19.0
Main armament	D10-TG	D10-T2S	U5-T	Rapira 3
Gun calibre (mm)	100	100	115	125
Stabilisation	1 plane	2 plane	2 plane	2 plane
Gun elevation (degrees)	$-5 +18$	$-5 +18$	$-3 +17$	—
Standard ammo stowage (total)	34	43	40	40
APHE	11	(15)	—	—
HEAT	6	7	6	6
HE	17	21	14	22
APDS/APFSDS	—	(15)	20	12
Co-axial machine gun 7.62mm	SGMT	SGMT	PKT	PKT
A/A machine gun 12.7mm	DShK	DShK	DShK	NSVT
Commander's sight	TPK-1	TPKU-2B	TKN-3	
Gunner's sight	TShA-2-22	TShB-2-22	TSh2B-414	TPD-2
Driver's IR sight	TVN-2	TVN-2	TVN-2	—
Smoke generator	BDSh-5	TDA	TDA	TDA
NBC protection	—	PAZ	PAZ	PAZ
Max. turret armour (mm)	210	210	170	275
Glacis armour (mm)	100	100	100	200
Hull armour (mm)	80	70	70	70

camouflage seems to have been confined to the use of mud swabbed over the tank. In most cases the mud seems to have been deliberately smeared over all unit insignia except for the British-style squadron sign on the turret side and on the fuel drum. The inset drawing shows the bridging circle carried on the front right fender. Some Indian tanks also had a white or yellow circle painted on the forward portion of the turret roof as an air identification marking.

B2: Type 59, A Squadron, Pakistani 11th Cavalry; Indo-Pakistan War, 1971

Pakistani armour in 1971 was regularly pattern-painted, usually with grey over dark green. In addition, a white band was painted around the turret to distinguish their tanks from Indian tanks.

Ethiopian troops inspect a Somali T-55A(M) knocked out near Dira Dawa on 10 March 1978 during the Ogaden War.

The barrel markings would appear to be troop markings, and the pennant in squadron colours; th turret number is '18'. A bridging circle is carried o the front left fender, and on the centre of the hull an arm-of-service flash in red and yellow. The seria follows the old British Far East pattern, with th number preceded by an upward-pointing arrow.

C1: T-55(M), Syrian 17th Mechanised Brigade Kuneitra, 1967

Syrian tanks in 1967 were basically left in their original Soviet dark green, although some had mu smeared over them. The markings consist of a whit circle (shown also in inset) for air identification, an the number '95451' on the glacis plate in Arabi numerals. Many Syrian tanks had honorary name painted on the turret sides, usually those of soldier who distinguished themselves in the 1948 war wit Israel. In this case the inscription is 'To the Marty Abraheem'.

A small portion of the tank haul by Israeli troops during the 1982 fighting in Lebanon. These are Syrian T-62s and T-62As captured during the fighting in the Bekaa Valley and around Beirut. The turrets are marked with the standard three-digit tactical number in Arabic script. (IDF)

2: Ti-67 of an Israeli tank brigade; Sinai front, 1973 War

During the 1973 War at least one Israeli tank brigade used the modified Ti-67s. The markings, in standard Israeli practice, consisted of a canvas panel with (in this case) 'Aleph-2' painted on it, indicating the second tank of the 1st Platoon. The usual company chevron insignia is not present on this tank. On the rear is a fluorescent orange air identification panel. The inset to the right shows a marking applied to some Soviet tanks used by the Israelis in 1973, presumably to distinguish them easily from hostile tanks.

1: Type 62 of a Chinese tank battalion; Sino-Vietnamese War, 1979

Chinese tanks are painted in an overall dark chrome green. The red and yellow national insignia regularly carried on the turret ahead of the three-digit tactical number. The inset drawings from left to right show the Kampuchean, Vietnamese and Chinese national insignia as used on their tanks.

D2: T-55(M) of a Libyan tank battalion, 1981

Libyan armour is painted in a bewildering variety of camouflage patterns, but this vehicle is simply in overall sand colour. The name on the turret side is that of the great 12th-century Arab leader Saladin. The only other standard marking is the licence plate, with 'army' written in Arabic above the vehicle number in Arabic script.

E1: T-54(mod), Maj. Saad Haddad's militia; Sidon, Lebanon, 1982

These refurbished T-54s were turned over to Haddad's militia in 1982. They are finished in grey-over-sand camouflage, but do not appear to carry the white St. Andrew's cross normally seen on Haddad's vehicles. The added stowage bins are very prominent in this view, as are the American M2 .50cal. and Browning .30cal. machine guns substituted for the Soviet weapons.

A Tanzanian Type 62 passes Tanzanian infantry during the advance into Uganda which toppled the regime of Idi Amin in April 1979. The Tanzanian tank battalion was built around Chinese Type 59 medium tanks and Type 62 light tanks like this one. The Type 62 can be distinguished from the similar Type 59 by its narrower track, different wheels, and smaller gun barrel.

E2: T-55(M) of an Iraqi tank regiment; Basra, Iran-Iraq War, 1982

Most Iraqi tanks appear to be camouflaged in sand and black, although this vehicle has added bands of rust red. The most unusual feature on this vehicle is the added skirts, which are rather reminiscent of those carried on some Bundeswehr vehicles.

F1: T-62A of an Afghan tank regiment; Afghanistan, 1982

Prior to the overthrow of Daoud by the Khalq Party under Taraki, Afghan tanks carried a national insignia consisting of a white circle with a triangle in the national colours. It would appear that this was not replaced with the current red circular insignia until after the Soviet-led overthrow

of Amin, and his replacement by Kamal. Th current insignia is a red disc, sometimes with th national crest painted over it.

F2: T-62, Soviet 11th Guards Tank Division; GSF(1980

This T-62 departs from the usually bland Sovi markings with a host of manoeuvre parad markings. The large turret slogan is 'Revolutionar Mongolia', a reference to the fact that the division Second World War antecedent, the 11th Guard Tank Corps, used tanks mostly purchased b contributions from Mongolia. In fact the regimer that this tank belongs to is called the 'Suche Bato Regiment, after the Mongolian hero. The Guard emblem is painted on the L-2G IR searchligl cover, and on the hull front are two of the regiment decorations, the Order of Bohdan Khemilnitskiy t the left and the Order of Victory to the right. Sovi tanks are painted in a very dark green (FS 3409 which is somewhat faded on this vehicle.

G1: T-62A, Syrian 81st Independent Tank Brigade; Golan Heights, 1973 War

This tank was initially finished in the usual Syrian scheme for the period of dark green with sand and medium grey patches. (This scheme is illustrated in Vanguard 19, *Armour of the Middle East Wars*, Plate G2.) However, this unit was stationed in the mountains north of Damascus, and had this swirling pattern of white added for winter camouflage. The brigade retained this scheme during the October fighting.

G2: T-62 of an Egyptian armoured brigade; Libyan border incident, 1979

Egyptian tanks serving on the Libyan frontier appear to have bands painted in the '8-10 o'clock', '2-4 o'clock' and '5-7 o'clock' positions of the turret as a means to distinguish them from identical Libyan tank types. Two white bands are also painted on the front fenders. This vehicle is camouflaged in the usual scheme of sand and field drab.

Ugandan T-55s parade in Kampala in February 1978. Uganda had about 15 of these during the fighting, but most were abandoned by their crews.

H1: T-72, Algerian armoured brigade, 1981

Algerian tanks are usually camouflaged with bands of dark green over sand. The turret numbers ('819' in this case) are carried centrally on the left turret side, and on the rear of the '5 o'clock' storage bin on the right side. The only national insignia is the small green and white circle on the serial box, shown in inset. The illustration shows the gill armour panels extended outward as they would appear in combat.

H2: T-72 of a Czechoslovak tank regiment; Druzhba manoeuvres, 1981

This illustration shows a CSA T-72 in the usual winter camouflage scheme. Whitewash bands have been applied in no particular system over the standard dark green finish. These vehicles did not appear to carry the usual three-digit white turret numbers, but did carry the national tricolour in the usual location.

Les notes sur les planches en couleur

A1 Les Tchèques sont la seule armée du Pacte de Varsovie à peindre régulièrement leurs chars dans des camouflages multicolores. Les peintures sur le détail de gravure montrent les insignes nationaux tchèque (à gauche) et polonais (à droite) sur des chars. **A2** Le pennon porte les couleurs de la compagnie—noir, rouge ou vert pour les 1ère, 2ème et 3ème compagnies—ainsi que l'emblème à trois flèches jaunes du Corps Blindé.

B1 Le camouflage est en fait de la boue étalée sur la peinture de base verte et sur la plupart des marques, au nombre desquelles se trouve l'insigne d'escadron de style britannique. Le canon du fusil est muni d'une boîte en fer blanc située à mi-longueur, permettant de distinguer les T-55 indiens des T-59 pakistanais. **B2** Camouflage peint en gris et vert; numéro de tourelle '18'; bande blanche autour de la tourelle permettant d'identifier rapidement les chars pakistanais; et apparemment les bandes blanches autour du canon de fusil servaient à identifier le peloton dans l'escadron.

C1 Le nom peint sur la tourelle est 'Le martyr Abraheem'. L'anneau blanc peint sur le toit de la tourelle servait à l'identification aérienne nationale. **C2** La toile porte la marque 'Aleph-2', indiquant qu'il s'agit du 2ème char du 1er Peloton. On peut voir sur la droite une marque trouvée sur quelques chars russes dans l'armée israélienne en 1973.

D1 L'insigne national est peint normalement sur la tourelle avec un numéro d'identification à trois chiffres. Le détail des peintures montre les insignes nationaux sur les chars du Kampouchéa, du Vietnam et de Chine. **D2** Les Lybiens utilisent des motifs différents de camouflage qui présentent une grande variété. Sur la tourelle de ce char est inscrit le nom 'Saladin'.

E1 Notez les coffres de rangement et les mitrailleuses ajoutés à ces chars par les Israéliens avant qu'ils soient fournis à la milice du Commandant Haddad. La croix blanche de St André n'apparaît pas sur ce char alors qu'on la trouvait normalement sur les véhicules d'Haddad. **E2** La plupart des chars iraquiens ont un camouflage couleur sable avec du noir, quoique celui-ci ait aussi des endroits couleur rouille.

F1 On peut voir l'insigne national courant, tel qu'il est utilisé depuis le renversement du régime d'Amin par Kamal. **F2** Des insignes supplémentaires ont été peints sur ce char destiné à un rassemblement. L'inscription sur la tourelle est 'Mongolie révolutionnaire'. L'emblème des Gardes est peint sur le couvercle de projecteur; et l'on peut voir sur l'avant de la coque deux décorations parmi celles remportées par le *Suche Bator Regt.*: il s'agit de l'Ordre de *Bodan Khemilnitskiy* et de l'Ordre de la Victoire.

G1 Ce camouflage blanc était ajouté en hiver sur le motif syrien courant en vert, sable et gris; il a été conservé pendant la guerre du mois d'octobre 1973. **G2** Des bandes blanches inscrites sur la tourelle en positions horaires, de 2 à 4 h, de 5 à 7 h et de 8 à 10 h servent à distinguer les chars égyptiens de ceux de leurs ennemis potentiels de l'autre côté de la frontière lybienne.

H1 Les numéros de tourelle sont peints au centre du côté gauche, ainsi que sur l'arrière du coffre de rangment qui se trouve sur le côté droit. **H2** Un camouflage temporaire d'hiver a été ajouté sur le vert foncé standard, masquant les numéros blancs que l'on peut voir normalement sur la tourelle; l'insigne national est conservé.

Farbtafeln

A1 Die Tschechoslowakei hat die einzige Armee unter den Staaten des Warschauer Paktes, die Panzer mit mehrfarbiger Kamouflage bemalt. Auf der Detailzeichnung sind tschechische (links) und polnische (rechts) Landeszeichen auf Panzern zu sehen. **A2** Der Wimpel hat die Kompaniefarben Schwarz, Rot oder Grün für die 1., 2. und 3. Kompanie und trägt das Emblem für das Bewaffnete Korps, drei gelbe Pfeile.

B1 Die Kamouflage ist aus Schlamm, der über die grüne Grundfarbe und die meisten Markierungen geschmiert wurde. Verdeckt sind unter anderem Geschwaderabzeichen, die den britischen ähnlich sind. Der Gewehrlauf hat auf halber Länge eine Blechdose, um die indischen T-55 von den pakistanischen T-59 zu unterscheiden. **B2** Graue und grüne aufgemalte Kamouflage; Kanzel-Nummer '18'; ein weisser Streifen rund um die Kanzel, um eine schnelle Identifizierung eines pakistanischen Panzers zu ermöglichen; ausserdem anscheinend weisse Streifen um den Gewehrlauf, um den Zug innerhalb des Geschwaders zu identifizieren.

C1 Der auf der Kanzel aufgemalte Name lautet 'Der Märtyrer Abraheem'. Der auf dem Kanzeldach aufgemalte weisse Ring dient zur Identifizierung der Nationalität aus der Luft. **C2** Das Tuch trägt die markierung 'Aleph-2', d.h. zweiter Panzer des 1. Zugs. Rechts sieht man eine Markierung, die 1973 auf einigen russischen Panzern in israelischem Einsatz beobachtet wurde.

D1 Das Landesabzeichen ist normalerweise mit einer dreistelligen Identitätsnummer auf der Kanzel aufgemalt. Die Detailzeichnung zeigt Landesabzeichen aus Kambodscha, Vietnam und China. **D2** Die Libyer benutzen viele verschiedene Kamouflagemuster. Dieser Panzer hat den Kanzelnamen 'Saladin'.

E1 Man beachte die Staukästen und MG, die Israel diesen Panzern hinzufügte, bevor sie an Major Haddads Truppen ausgegeben wurden. Bei diesem Panzer fehlt das weisse Andreaskreuz, das Haddads Fahrzeuge gewöhnlich tragen. **E2** Die meisten irakischen Panzer haben sandfarbene und schwarze Kamouflage; dieser hat auch rostfarbene Flächen.

F1 Hier abgebildet ist das zur Zeit benutzte Landesabzeichen, das seit dem Sturz des Amin-Regimes durch Kamal gültig ist. **F2** Auf diesen Panzer wurden für eine Parade zusätzliche Abzeichen aufgemalt. Die Aufschrift auf der Kanzel bedeutet 'Revolutionäre Mongolei'; das Garde-Emblem ist auf die Suchscheinwerferhülle gemalt; auf der Vorderseite der Karosserie sind zwei vom Suche Bator Regt. gewonnenen Auszeichnungen abgebildet: der Bohdan Khemilnitskij-Orden und der Siegesorden.

G1 Für den Winter wurde diese weisse Tarnfarbe über das syrische Kamouflagemuster Grün, Sandfarben und Grau gemalt; sie wurde für den Oktoberkrieg 1973 beibehalten. **G2** Weisse Streifen auf der Kanzel in den Positionen '2 vor 4', '5 vor 7' und '8 vor 10 Uhr' unterscheiden die ägyptischen Panzer von ihren potentiellen Feinden jenseits der libyschen Grenze.

H1 Kanzelnummern sind in der Mitte der linken Seite ausgemalt und auf die hintere Oberfläche des rechten Staukastens. **H2** Eine vorübergehend benutzte Winter-Kamouflage über dem normalen Dunkelgrün, die die sonst auf der Kanzel sichtbaren Zahlen überdeckt; das Landesabzeichen ist beibehalten.